WHY EASTER?

Barbara Reaoch

illustrated by carol mccarty

Shepherd Press

M000273761

Why Easter?
©2012 by Barbara Reaoch
Illustrated by Carol McCarty
Page design, typesetting, cover design by Tobias' Outerwear for Books

ISBN: 978-1-936908-31-8

ISBN Mobi: 978-1-936908-32-5
ISBN ePub: 978-1-936908-33-2

Published by Shepherd Press
P.O. Box 24
Wapwallopen, Pennsylvania 18660

All rights reserved. No part of this book may be reproduced or utilized in any
form or by any means, electronic or mechanical, or by any information storage and retrieval system—except for brief
quotations for the purpose of review, without written permission from the publisher.
Unless otherwise indicated, all Scripture are taken from *The Holy Bible*, English Standard Version. Copyright ©2001 by
Crossway Bibles, a division of Good News Publishers. Used by permission. All rights reserved.

Italics or bold text within Scripture quotations indicate emphasis added by author.

First Printing, 2012
Printed in the United States of America

Library of Congress Cataloging-in-Publication Data

Reaoch, Barbara.
  Why Easter? / Barbara Reaoch ; illustrated by Carol McCarty.
    p. cm.
  ISBN 978-1-936908-31-8 (print book : alk. paper) -- ISBN 978-1-936908-32-5
(kindle e-book) -- ISBN 978-1-936908-33-2 (epub e-book)
  1. Easter--Study and teaching. 2. Jesus Christ--Study and teaching. 3.
Families--Religious life. 4. Devotional literature. I. Title.
  BV55.R38 2012
  249--dc23
                    2011052501

Get an eBook of *Why Easter?* at http://www.shepherdpress.com/ebooks

Kindle: EasterK
ePub: EasterE

JOS 22 21 20 19 18 17 16 15 14 13 12
14 13 12 11 10 9 8 7 6 5 4 3 2 1

To our grandchildren, Milaina, Noah, Annalyse, Toph and those yet to be born, that you may know "the praiseworthy deeds of the Lord, His power, and the wonders He has done." (Psalm 78:4)

Start reading *Why Easter*? at any time of the year. However, to prepare your family for a meaningful celebration of Easter, start reading four weeks before the calendar date. Stick with a daily plan for family devotions—it will be worth it. Using this devotion before Easter could be the start of a significant tradition for your family.

How to Use this Devotional

Pray God wants us to know Him and His plan for us through Jesus Christ so He has given us His Word. Start by asking God to help everyone listen and understand what you are about to read.

Read This is the vital part of your devotional time. Engaging with God's Word every day is key for God's children. Read the Scripture references from the Bible to emphasize to your child that God speaks to us through His Word. Shorten or lengthen the Bible reading according to your child's attention span, but do not leave this part out. Even when you have limited time for devotions read God's Word.

Listen These short comments will help you explain God's Word to your child.

Truth Stating the truth will help your child know what the Scripture teaches about God and His plan.

Discuss Asking good questions stimulates the mind and heart. Engage your child in discussion and encourage application of God's Word to everyday life.

Memorize Children have a great capacity for memorization. The memory verses in *Why Easter?* are a presentation of the Gospel. Your child will know the Gospel after memorizing these verses. Read and memorize one verse (printed in color) each day so that the entire passage is memorized at the end of the week.

Sing Children love to sing. Do not let a lack of confidence keep you from enjoying this part. Hymns reinforce the truths of Christ's death and resurrection. Clarifying some of the words will make the hymn a meaningful lifelong favorite. The words for the hymns are at the back of the book. Use a hymnal or hymnal website to become familiar with the music.

Read: John 11:17–27 and 38–44

Listen: Who are your good friends? Lazarus, Mary, and Martha were very good friends of Jesus. This was a sad time for them but Jesus wanted to teach his friends something important. When God created the world, everything was good. God made the first people, Adam and Eve, and gave them a home with Him in a beautiful place called Eden. Then one day everything changed. Adam and Eve did not obey the rules that God made for them. They wanted to do things their own way. They disobeyed God. This is called sin. Their punishment was to leave beautiful Eden, forever. No longer did they talk with God and enjoy His friendship with them. Life outside Eden was hard. Then one day Adam and Eve died.

Adam was the first father on the earth. We all come from Adam and Eve, and every person born after Adam is like him. We all tend to do what we want instead of obeying God (Rom. 5:18-19). God loves us very much, and it is wrong for us to disobey Him. It is right and it is fair for God to punish us for sin. We all have the same punishment as Adam. Is there any hope for us to enjoy a friendship with God? Jesus told Lazarus, Mary and Martha (and us) something important about God's plan.

God loves you and planned for Jesus to take your punishment. Jesus came back to life after He died and now lives in heaven. Boys, girls, moms and dads, those who believe Jesus took the punishment for their sin are God's children. God's children enjoy a friendship with Him. They live with God forever. Although their body may die on earth, they will live in heaven and one day be given a new body. Jesus raised Lazarus to life, and He has the power to give you the new life He promised.

Truth: God planned for Jesus to take our punishment for sin.

Discuss:

1. What do all people want to do instead of obeying God?

2. What is the punishment for sin?

3. What does Jesus promise for those who believe in Him?

Memorize: Week 1–Acts 2:22-24

• **Day 1—Acts 2:22**

22 "Men of Israel, hear these words: Jesus of Nazareth, a man attested to you by God with mighty works and wonders and signs that God did through him in your midst, as you yourselves know— 23this Jesus, delivered up according to the definite plan and foreknowledge of God, you crucified and killed by the hands of lawless men. 24 God raised him up, loosing the pangs of death, because it was not possible for him to be held by it.

• **Discuss verse 22:**
"Men of Israel, hear these words: Jesus of Nazareth, a man attested to you by God"

Sing: "When I Survey the Wondrous Cross" (p. 62)

• **Discuss "survey."**
Discuss what time each day this month you will read the Bible together and grow in your understanding of Jesus' life, death, and resurrection.

Read: John 12:1-8

Listen: How do we show Jesus our love for Him? Lazarus, Martha, and Mary were so grateful for all Jesus had done. Lazarus had died but now he was alive. Jesus did what no one else could do. Lazarus wanted to show Jesus his love. He honored Jesus with a special dinner. Martha started to prepare to serve all of Jesus' favorite food to show her love for Him. How would Mary show Jesus her love?

The day came for Jesus and His friends to gather around the table with Lazarus. The freshly baked bread smelled good and everyone was hungry. Martha happily served the guests and had decided to serve Jesus the rest of her life. Suddenly the aroma of freshly baked bread was overpowered by a sweet fragrance. What was it? All eyes were on Mary as she poured perfume on Jesus' feet. This was no ordinary perfume. It had cost what one person earned in a whole year of work. In those days people poured this kind of perfume over the body of a loved one when they died.

Mary had always listened closely to Jesus as He spoke. Mary heard Jesus talk about death as the awful penalty of sin. When Lazarus died, Mary felt the sting of this truth. However, Mary heard Jesus call Himself the resurrection and the life and that He was the way for a person to be forgiven of sin and live forever with God. In pouring this perfume on Jesus, Mary was telling Jesus she believed Him. She trusted Jesus and knew what He said was true. Mary showed her love for Jesus by believing Him.

Was Mary wasting her money? Judas thought so. Judas wanted the money for himself (Luke 12:16-21). Judas heard Jesus talk many times, but did not believe Him (Matt. 26:14-16). Many people are like Judas. They hear about Jesus but do not believe what He says. Mary understood Jesus and believed Him (Matt. 13:23).

Truth: Jesus gave His life so we can be forgiven.

Discuss:

1. What did Mary believe about Jesus?

2. What will you do to listen closely to Jesus' words?

3. How will you show your love for Jesus today?

Memorize: Week 1–Acts 2:22-24

• Day 2—Acts 2:22

22"Men of Israel, hear these words: Jesus of Nazareth, a man attested to you by God with mighty works and wonders and signs that God did through him in your midst, as you yourselves know— 23this Jesus, delivered up according to the definite plan and foreknowledge of God, you crucified and killed by the hands of lawless men. 24God raised him up, loosing the pangs of death, because it was not possible for him to be held by it.

• Discuss verse 22:
"with mighty works and wonders and signs that God did through him in your midst, as you yourselves know"

Sing: "When I Survey the Wondrous Cross" (p. 62)

• Discuss "my richest gain."
What is my richest gain compared with the love of Jesus?

Read: John 12:12–18 and Matthew 21:15–17

week 1 · Day 3

Listen: "Here he comes! Here he comes," shouted the children. They looked up from their games and saw Jesus coming toward Jerusalem. "Let's go tell our family and friends so they can come and see this famous man," they said. By now, everyone knew that Jesus had raised Lazarus from the dead. They were sure Jesus was the Messiah-King that God had promised to send. A crowd quickly gathered. They spread coats and palm branches down on the rocky, dusty road so Jesus would know He was honored (Matt. 21:8). From the Scriptures they knew that the Messiah-King would come from the family line of King David.

As Jesus got closer, they started shouting "Hosanna to the son of David!" Hosanna means "save now." The children were so excited and kept saying "Hosanna to the Son of David, Hosanna to the Son of David" (Matt. 21:15-16). The adults were also overjoyed and said, "Finally we will be free from Roman rule." The Roman government made laws that made life hard for the Jewish people. They thought God's King (Messiah) was coming to give them freedom from the Roman government.

The people also knew that the Scriptures told of the Messiah-King riding into Jerusalem on a donkey (Zech. 9:9). Why would the Messiah-King not ride a horse? All kings rode horses to show their strength for battle. Jesus was different from other kings. Jesus was stronger than any other king but He followed God's plan in humility. He came to save the people from something much worse than a government that made life hard. He came to save them from their sin.

Truth: Jesus is the Messiah-King God promised to send.

Discuss:

1. Why did the people put coats and palm branches on the road?

2. Why did the people shout, "Hosanna to the son of David"?

3. Why did Jesus ride a donkey and not a horse?

Memorize: Week 1–Acts 2:22-24

• Day 3—Acts 2:23

22 "Men of Israel, hear these words: Jesus of Nazareth, a man attested to you by God with mighty works and wonders and signs that God did through him in your midst, as you yourselves know— **23this Jesus, delivered up according to the definite plan and foreknowledge of God, you crucified and killed by the hands of lawless men.** *24 God raised him up, loosing the pangs of death, because it was not possible for him to be held by it.*

• Discuss verse 23:
"this Jesus, delivered up"

Sing: "When I Survey the Wondrous Cross" (p. 62)

• Discuss "Prince of Glory."
What does it mean to be a Prince or King?

Listen: Children loved Jesus. He taught them true stories about God and they knew Jesus was the Messiah King that God had promised to send (Matt. 11:25-26). Why did the religious leaders hate Jesus so much? (Luke 19:47).

The day Jesus came into the temple the religious leaders thought, "Who is this Jesus coming in like he owns the place and turning over our tables?" As coins rolled out of sight, birds flew off, and animals got loose, they were angry. Passover was when the religious leaders made most of their money. When rich and poor people came to Jerusalem for the Passover they bought an animal or bird for the Passover sacrifice. And each person had to pay a tax for the upkeep of the temple. The temple tax was paid with Jewish money. When people did not have Jewish money they exchanged their money for Jewish money. The religious leaders charged people too much money in the exchange. This is why Jesus called them robbers. Jesus was angry that these men were stealing from the people when they should have been leading them closer to God.

The religious leaders hated Jesus for many reasons. They were jealous that the people loved Him. They did not want to believe that Jesus was the Messiah-King. And they did not like it when Jesus talked about the sin that was in their hearts, so they planned to kill Jesus.

Truth: Jesus is the Messiah-King that God promised to send.

Discuss:

1. Why did all the people come to Jerusalem?

2. Why was Jesus angry?

3. Why were the religious leaders angry with Jesus?

Memorize: Week 1–Acts 2:22-24

• **Day 4—Acts 2:23**

22"*Men of Israel, hear these words: Jesus of Nazareth, a man attested to you by God with mighty works and wonders and signs that God did through him in your midst, as you yourselves know—* 23**this Jesus, delivered up according to the definite plan and foreknowledge of God, you crucified and killed by the hands of lawless men.** 24*God raised him up, loosing the pangs of death, because it was not possible for him to be held by it.*

• **Discuss verse 23:**
 "according to the definite plan and foreknowledge of God"

Sing: "When I Survey the Wondrous Cross" (p. 62)

• **Discuss "all the vain things that charm me most."**
What are some vain things that charm you most?

Listen: "Hurry, hurry," the children called to their friends. "Jesus is coming to tell us true stories about God." After Jesus chased the money changers out of the temple He sat down with the people. When they listened to Jesus, they knew He was teaching them the very Word of God.

The religious leaders' teaching was different. They added rules to God's commandments. God gave us commandments for us to know Him. God gave commandments for us to know what He requires of us. Was it right for the religious leaders to add more rules to God's commandments? The people wondered which rules were the most important to obey so they listened closely to Jesus' answer.

They may have thought, "I can do that, I can love God and I can love my neighbor." However, when Jesus said we are to love God with all our heart, soul, mind and strength they realized that was not possible. Even when they tried hard to think about God and love Him all day, they could not. They could work to help their neighbor, but there were times when unkind thoughts about that person filled their minds. No one can always keep God's commands without ever disobeying. Will God forgive us? God in His great mercy planned for Jesus to take the punishment we deserve. God will give us a new heart so we want to obey Him. God will give us His Spirit so we have the power to say "no" to sin.

Truth: God's commandments tell us about His love and requirements.

Discuss:

1. What did Jesus say is the most important commandment?

2. Have you tried to keep God's commandments? What happened?

3. What do you learn about God from His commandments?

Memorize: Week 1–Acts 2:22-24

• Day 5—Acts 2:23

*22"Men of Israel, hear these words: Jesus of Nazareth, a man attested to you by God with mighty works and wonders and signs that God did through him in your midst, as you yourselves know— 23**this Jesus, delivered up according to the definite plan and foreknowledge of God, you crucified and killed by the hands of lawless men.** 24God raised him up, loosing the pangs of death, because it was not possible for him to be held by it.*

• Discuss verse 23:
"you crucified and killed by the hands of lawless men."

Sing: "When I Survey the Wondrous Cross" (p. 62)

• Discuss "boast."
What is the difference between boasting about yourself and boasting about Christ?

Read: matthew 26:1–5

Listen: "Stop pushing," a boy said to his brother. "We can see Jesus from here." People crowded into the temple to hear Jesus teach. Thousands of people were in Jerusalem to celebrate the Passover.

Where were all the religious leaders? They were in the palace of the high priest for a special meeting. "How will we stop Jesus?" the religious leaders wondered. They did not like it when Jesus was in the temple and felt that they were not in control when Jesus was teaching. They started to plan how to kill Jesus but decided to wait until after the Passover crowds left Jerusalem. The people would not like their plan.

God also had a plan. Jesus took His friends, the disciples, aside and told them that in two days He would be killed. Jesus had always slipped away before they could catch Him. This time was different because it was time for Jesus to do what His Father had planned (John 4:34). The religious leaders thought they were in control of the plans for Jesus' death, but God was in control. Jesus knew the prophet Isaiah had described His death (Isa. 53). God's power to carry out His plan is greater than man's power. God planned for Jesus to die to take the punishment for sin. God planned for Jesus to die at Passover.

Truth: Jesus knew it was God's plan for Him to die at Passover.

Discuss:

1. Why did the religious leaders want to kill Jesus?

2. When did the religious leaders plan to kill Jesus?

3. How was God's plan different from the plan of the religious leaders?

Memorize: Week 1–Acts 2:22-24

• **Day 6—Acts 2:24**

22"*Men of Israel, hear these words: Jesus of Nazareth, a man attested to you by God with mighty works and wonders and signs that God did through him in your midst, as you yourselves know—* 23*this Jesus, delivered up according to the definite plan and foreknowledge of God, you crucified and killed by the hands of lawless men.* 24 **God raised him up, loosing the pangs of death, because it was not possible for him to be held by it.***

• **Discuss verse 24:**
"God raised him up, loosing the pangs of death."

Sing: "When I Survey the Wondrous Cross" (p. 62)

• **Discuss "love and sorrow meet."**
How did Jesus have love and sorrow in His death?

read: matthew 26:17-19

Listen: Why was Passover a favorite celebration for the Jewish people? At Passover, the people remembered how God had once saved them from slavery in Egypt. One night in Egypt a long time ago, God told the Jewish people to put the blood of a lamb over their door. The Lord would "pass over" the houses with the blood over the door (Ex. 12).

God is right and fair in giving a very serious punishment for sin. God is the Creator and everything belongs to Him. He loves us and it is wrong for us to want to be in charge of our life instead of obeying Him (Rom. 3:10-11). The punishment for sin is death. In God's mercy, He allows a substitute to take the punishment for the person who has sinned. In the Old Testament, God planned for a lamb to be the substitute for sinners. A substitute takes the place of some other person or thing like a substitute teacher takes the place of another teacher at school. At Passover, the blood of the lamb over the door meant that the lamb was the substitute sacrifice for the sins of the people in that house. God made a way for sin to be punished and sinners to be saved.

The substitute sacrifice of lambs in the Old Testament is the picture for us of Jesus the Lamb of God who takes away the sin of the world (John 1:29). The lamb chosen for the sacrifice had to be perfect without any spot or blemish. Jesus was the only One who ever obeyed all of God's commands all the time. Jesus never sinned (1 Peter 1:18-19). Since Jesus had no sin of His own, He was able to be the perfect substitute.

Jesus was willing to take the punishment for sin that we deserve (Heb. 9:26). Jesus did this when He died on the cross and took all the terrible anger that God has toward sin. Because of this, God's people are saved so they can live forever with God. When a boy, girl, mom, or dad trusts Jesus, they are forgiven by God and have the joy of living with Him forever.

Truth: Jesus took the punishment for sin.

Discuss:

1. Why was Passover a favorite holiday for the Jewish people?

2. What is sin and why is it so serious?

3. Why is Jesus called the Lamb of God?

Memorize: Week 1–Acts 2:22-24

• Day 7—Acts 2:24

²²"*Men of Israel, hear these words: Jesus of Nazareth, a man attested to you by God with mighty works and wonders and signs that God did through him in your midst, as you yourselves know—* ²³*this Jesus, delivered up according to the definite plan and foreknowledge of God, you crucified and killed by the hands of lawless men.* ²⁴**God raised him up, loosing the pangs of death, because it was not possible for him to be held by it.***

• Discuss verse 24:
"because it was not possible for him to be held by it."

Sing: "When I Survey the Wondrous Cross" (p. 62)

• Discuss "pride."
What does it mean to pour contempt on all my pride?

Listen: Jesus knew everything that was going to happen. He knew the exact place where He would eat the Passover meal with His friends, the disciples. The Passover meal was the beginning of the Feast of Unleavened Bread. When God gave the Jewish people instructions for the Passover meal He told them to make bread without leaven. What is leaven? Leaven makes the bread rise. Leaven is a picture of evil, and God did not want them to have any evil in their houses or hearts. Before they applied the blood of the lamb over the door of their house and ate the Passover meal, they were to get rid of everything that was evil. And before Jesus ate the Passover meal with His friends, He got rid of the evil in the room.

The disciples were alarmed when Jesus said that one of them was going to betray Him. How could one of the disciples help Jesus' enemies arrest Him? Each disciple thought, "Could Jesus be speaking of me?" Jesus had just told them the truth about the pride in their hearts (Mark 9:33-35 and 10:35-45). They realized that Jesus knew them better than they knew themselves. They did not want any sin to keep them from Jesus' love.

Judas was different. He had been with Jesus a long time but did not believe what Jesus taught. When Judas heard Jesus' warning, he did not ask Jesus to forgive him. Without Jesus' forgiveness, Judas would have to take the horrible punishment for his own sin. When Judas died, he would not be with God in heaven. Judas would be in a place of pain and sadness, far, far away from God. The Bible calls this awful place "hell."

Truth: Jesus knows everything before it happens.

Discuss:

1. Why did the Jewish people eat bread without leaven?

2. What did Jesus know was about to happen?

3. Why should a person ask for Jesus' forgiveness?

Memorize: Week 2–Acts 2:29-31

• Day 8—Acts 2:29

29"Brothers, I may say to you with confidence about the patriarch David that he both died and was buried, and his tomb is with us to this day. *30 Being therefore a prophet, and knowing that God had sworn with an oath to him that he would set one of his descendants on his throne, 31he foresaw and spoke about the resurrection of the Christ, that he was not abandoned to Hades, nor did his flesh see corruption.*

• Discuss verse 29:
"Brothers, I may say to you with confidence about the patriarch David."

Sing: "Man of Sorrows! What a Name" (p. 63)

• Discuss "ruined sinner."
What does it mean that Jesus reclaims ruined sinners?

read: matthew 26:26-30

Listen: What did Jesus do after Judas left to find the religious leaders? Jesus wanted His disciples to understand that this was the last time they would celebrate the Passover. Why? Passover was a time to remember that long ago God saved them from Egyptian slavery. Something new and greater was about to happen. Instead of a lamb taking the punishment that God requires, Jesus was going to take the punishment and shed his blood for our forgiveness (1 Cor. 5:7). The blood of the Passover lamb was not needed any more as the punishment for sin (Heb. 10:4).

Why is blood needed for the forgiveness of sin? (Heb. 9:22). It is the blood inside a creature that gives it life, and the punishment for sin is death (Lev. 17:14). Why did the lamb have to be without any flaw? The perfect lamb was a picture of Jesus who never sinned (Heb. 9:15). Jesus is the "Lamb of God" who takes away the sin of the world (John 1:29). God's love is so great that He made a way for us to be forgiven through the blood of Jesus (See 2 Cor. 5:21).

Instead of eating the Passover meal and remembering that God saved the people from slavery in Egypt, Jesus said to eat His supper (the Lord's Supper or Communion) and remember that He died to save us from being slaves to sin. When we eat the Lord's Supper, we remember God's love and Jesus' great sacrifice. As we remember Jesus' sacrifice, we also look forward to His return. Those who believe and trust Jesus will eat this supper with Him when He returns.

Truth: Jesus gave His life for the forgiveness of our sin.

Discuss:

1. Why is the Passover lamb no longer needed?

2. Why is blood required for the forgiveness of sin?

3. What are we to remember until Jesus returns?

Memorize: Week 2–Acts 2:29-31

• Day 9—Acts 2:29

29"Brothers, I may say to you with confidence about the patriarch David that he both died and was buried, and his tomb is with us to this day. 30 Being therefore a prophet, and knowing that God had sworn with an oath to him that he would set one of his descendants on his throne, 31he foresaw and spoke about the resurrection of the Christ, that he was not abandoned to Hades, nor did his flesh see corruption.

• Discuss verse 29:
"that he both died and was buried, and his tomb is with us to this day"

Sing: "Man of Sorrows! What a Name" (p. 63)

• Discuss: "Spotless Lamb of God" and "atonement" (at-one with God).

What does it mean that Jesus provided atonement?

Listen: When a shepherd sees a wolf coming, he warns his sheep with a loud whistle so they will run to safety. Just as a wolf comes to destroy sheep, the enemy of God, Satan, comes to attack God's children. Jesus knew that Satan was going to tempt His friends to sin in a way they had never known before (Luke 22:31) and He warned them of this danger.

Peter was a strong man. His body was strong from his hard work as a fisherman. Then his spirit became strong from being with Jesus. He learned about love from following Jesus even when it was hard to do. Jesus considered Peter one of His closest friends and a leader among the disciples. Yet had Peter begun to rely too much on his own strength?

Instead of listening to Jesus' warning, Peter said he would never stop being Jesus' friend. Instead of admitting any weakness, Peter thought he was stronger than the rest of the disciples. Instead of asking for Jesus' help, he thought he could overcome temptation on his own. Peter did not realize he had already fallen into sin because of the pride in his heart. Jesus wanted Peter to learn to call out for His help when tempted by Satan to do something wrong. With time, Peter would learn how to rely on Jesus for this kind of strength that overcomes temptation (1 Peter 5: 4-11). Peter had never felt more pain in his heart than when he sinned against Jesus. And Peter never felt more joy than when he received Jesus' forgiveness (John 21: 15-23).

Truth: Jesus' forgiveness gives joy and strength to overcome temptation.

Discuss:

1. What did Jesus know would happen to His friends?

2. What are ways that Satan tempts people to sin?

3. What have you learned about turning away from temptation?

Memorize: Week 2–Acts 2:29-31

• Day 10—Acts 2:30

[29]"Brothers, I may say to you with confidence about the patriarch David that he both died and was buried, and his tomb is with us to this day. [30] **Being therefore a prophet, and knowing that God had sworn with an oath to him that he would set one of his descendants on his throne,** [31]he foresaw and spoke about the resurrection of the Christ, that he was not abandoned to Hades, nor did his flesh see corruption.

• Discuss verse 30:
"Being therefore a prophet, and knowing that God had sworn with an oath to him"

Sing: "Man of Sorrows! What a Name" (p. 63)

• Discuss: "guilty, vile, and helpless."
How are we helpless and weak with regard to sin?

Listen: Jesus knew His friends wanted to do what was right but they did not have the strength (Mark 14:38). When have you wanted to share with your brother or sister and then selfishly kept the best for yourself? When have you wanted to obey your mother and then did what she said not to do? When have you wanted to tell a friend about Jesus and then felt too afraid?

Jesus knows how God's enemy, Satan, will tempt us (Matt. 4:1-11). Even though Jesus never sinned, He understands every temptation we will have. Jesus can help us not to sin because He is the only one who has never sinned (Heb. 4:15). Learning from Jesus to "watch and pray so that you will not fall into temptation" is important. Learning from Jesus' example as He faced the hardest temptation of His life is powerful.

Jesus knew to pray and ask God for the strength to do God's will. Dying on a cross was going to be very painful for Jesus. There was something even more painful for Him than the thorns and nails. Jesus who had never sinned would take all our sin upon Himself. Harder yet, Jesus knew His Father could not be close to sin and would not be near Him during that time. This was so hard for Jesus that He asked God if there was some other way to deal with our sin. When Jesus felt the weight of this temptation, He prayed and God gave Him strength to do His will.

Our temptation will not be as hard as Jesus' temptation, but we will be tempted to not do what God wants us to do. We are not strong or brave enough to do what God tells us to do. Jesus tells us to pray for God's help when we are tempted (Matt.6:13), and He promises to help us do what is right.

Truth: God gives strength to do His will.

Discuss:

1. What did Jesus do when He was tempted?

2. Why can Jesus give us strength not to sin when we are tempted?

3. With what temptation do you need God's strength?

Memorize: Week 2–Acts 2:29-31

• **Day 11—Acts 2:30**

29"Brothers, I may say to you with confidence about the patriarch David that he both died and was buried, and his tomb is with us to this day. **30 Being therefore a prophet, and knowing that God had sworn with an oath to him that he would set one of his descendants on his throne,** 31he foresaw and spoke about the resurrection of the Christ, that he was not abandoned to Hades, nor did his flesh see corruption.

• **Discuss verse 30:**
"that he would set one of his descendants on his throne"

Sing: "Man of Sorrows! What a Name" (p. 63)

• **Discuss "Man of sorrows."**
What caused Jesus sorrow when He lived on earth?

Listen: The disciples wondered, "Why are all these soldiers coming into the garden?" While Jesus was still talking a large crowd of soldiers and religious leaders came to capture Him. They had never before been able to catch Jesus (John 10:39). Therefore, expecting a fight, Jesus' enemies came with clubs and swords. The disciples were not ready for what happened next.

When a man grabbed Jesus, Peter grabbed his sword and cut off the man's ear. The soldiers, religious leaders and disciples all believed they were strong enough to win this fight but Jesus was the strongest of them all. Jesus' words were so powerful that the whole crowd fell to the ground when He spoke (John 18:6). With His power Jesus attached the soldier's ear back in place as if it had never been cut off (Luke 22:51). Because He had all authority over the angels in heaven, Jesus could have called an army of angels to help Him at any time.

However, Jesus did not use His strength to fight. He knew that God's plan was greater than the sinful plan of the people. Jesus let Judas kiss Him. Jesus let them capture Him. Jesus let all the disciples leave Him. Jesus had the strength to do everything God sent Him to do (John 18:11).

Truth: Jesus wanted to do everything God planned.

Discuss:

1. Why did the people bring clubs and swords to capture Jesus?

2. How strong is Jesus?

3. Why did Jesus not fight?

Memorize: Week 2–Acts 2:29-31

• Day 12—Acts 2:31

[29] *"Brothers, I may say to you with confidence about the patriarch David that he both died and was buried, and his tomb is with us to this day.* [30] *Being therefore a prophet, and knowing that God had sworn with an oath to him that he would set one of his descendants on his throne,* [31] ***he foresaw and spoke about the resurrection of the Christ, that he was not abandoned to Hades, nor did his flesh see corruption.***

• Discuss verse 31:
"he foresaw and spoke about the resurrection of the Christ"

Sing: "Man of Sorrows! What a Name" (p. 63)

• Discuss "bearing shame and scoffing rude."
What would have caused shame for Jesus in His arrest? How did Jesus react to the "scoffing rude" of the soldiers, Judas and his disciples?

Listen: When the soldiers tied Jesus' hands and took him away, all the disciples ran into the darkness. They did not want to be captured too. Jesus was led to the home of Annas who had once been the high priest. Annas was called high priest his whole life even though his son-in-law, Caiaphas, was the high priest at this time. A high priest led all the other religious leaders and performed religious duties in the temple. Annas was not a good leader of God's people. He cared more about making a profit from the money changing in the temple than teaching the people about God. Annas must have been angry when Jesus said the temple was a "den of robbers." Caiaphas said about Jesus that it was better that "one man die for the nation" (John 11:49-53). Annas agreed.

Jesus' trial with Annas was the first of six trials. When someone is accused of doing something wrong there is a trial to find out what is true. After the truth is known, the person on trial is guilty or not guilty of the accusations. However, the religious leaders were not interested in the truth about Jesus because they had already decided He should die. They did not have a legal reason to kill Jesus because Jesus had done nothing against the law.

The religious leaders knew it was important to follow the rules for a fair trial, but during Jesus' trials they did not follow these rules. They were not to have trials at night, yet it was probably about midnight when Annas began questioning Jesus. Trials were not to start before there was a clear accusation. The religious leaders did not have any accusation of Jesus. A trial was to take place in the temple where all the people could listen, but Jesus was taken away into the home of the high priest. If Annas wanted to know the truth about Jesus, he would have followed the rules for a fair trial.

Truth: Jesus had done nothing wrong.

Discuss:

1. What happened to the disciples when Jesus was taken away?

2. What kind of leader of God's people was Annas?

3. What did the religious leaders hope to find out during these trials?

Memorize: Week 2–Acts 2:29-31

• **Day 13—Acts 2:31**

[29]"Brothers, I may say to you with confidence about the patriarch David that he both died and was buried, and his tomb is with us to this day. [30] Being therefore a prophet, and knowing that God had sworn with an oath to him that he would set one of his descendants on his throne, [31]**he foresaw and spoke about the resurrection of the Christ, that he was not abandoned to Hades, nor did his flesh see corruption.**

• **Discuss verse 31:**
"that he was not abandoned to Hades"

Sing: "Man of Sorrows! What a Name" (p. 63)

• **Discuss "condemned" from "in my place condemned He stood."**
How was Jesus condemned in your place?

Listen: The people of Jerusalem were sleeping in the early morning hours when they took Jesus from Annas to the house of the high priest Caiaphas. Caiaphas had started planning to kill Jesus when Lazarus was raised from the dead (John 11:45-53). He did not like it when Jesus said that He was the Messiah. Now the whole Sanhedrin gathered to listen to Jesus' testimony. The Sanhedrin was a group of seventy-one religious leaders. They made legal decisions for the Jewish people and Caiaphas led their meetings.

In a fair trial witnesses tell the truth about what they have seen or heard about the person being accused. Caiaphas could not find anyone who had seen Jesus break the law. However, some people were willing to say things that were not true about Jesus. The two witnesses did not tell what Jesus really said. When Caiaphas heard what they said, he had an idea. If Caiaphas could get Jesus to say that He was the Messiah, they could accuse Him of blasphemy. Blasphemy is telling a lie about God. If someone who was not the Messiah said he was, he would be lying about God.

Why did Caiaphas tear his clothes when Jesus said, "Yes, I am the Messiah?" A priest never tore his clothes except when someone said something blasphemous. Caiaphas tore his clothes to make it seem that it was blasphemous of Jesus to say He was the Son of God (Messiah). But it was not blasphemous because Jesus was telling the truth. Caiaphas tore his clothes to make it seem like he was furious. However, he was actually glad that they now had an accusation against Jesus. The punishment for blasphemy was death.

Truth: Jesus was not guilty of any wrongdoing.

Discuss:

1. Did Caiaphas want to know the truth about Jesus?

2. What did Caiaphas want the witnesses to say about Jesus?

3. Why did Caiaphas tear his clothes?

Memorize: Week 2–Acts 2:29-31

• Day 14—Acts 2:31

29 "Brothers, I may say to you with confidence about the patriarch David that he both died and was buried, and his tomb is with us to this day. 30 Being therefore a prophet, and knowing that God had sworn with an oath to him that he would set one of his descendants on his throne, 31he foresaw and spoke about the resurrection of the Christ, that he was not abandoned to Hades, nor did his flesh see corruption.

• Discuss verse 31:
"nor did his flesh see corruption"

Sing: "Man of Sorrows! What a Name" (p. 63)

• Discuss "Hallelujah, what a Savior!"
What does it mean to say that Jesus is the Savior (Messiah)?

Listen: As the sun rose at the start of a new day, the religious leaders called the Sanhedrin to yet another meeting. The Sanhedrin wanted to keep the rule to make the final decision about a trial in daylight. However, they did not keep the rule that said a person on trial needed to be fairly treated and not hurt. Caiaphas let the religious leaders spit in Jesus' face (Mark 14:65). Others hit Jesus and slapped him (Matt. 26:67). The guards beat up Jesus and said bad things about Him (Luke 22:63).

Caiaphas and the Sanhedrin did not want to believe that Jesus was the Messiah. The religious leaders believed God was going to send the Messiah (Isa. 9:6-7), but they wanted a Messiah that said they were doing a good job. Jesus never said anything good about them. If Jesus' teaching was always different from their teaching, the people would stop listening to them. They wanted a Messiah that would make them stronger than the Roman government which was ruling their country. Jesus did not act like the Messiah the religious leaders were expecting.

Under Jewish law, the Sanhedrin had the right to request the death penalty for blasphemy. But since the Roman government was the ruling authority in Jerusalem, the Sanhedrin did not have the right to put anyone to death. If Jesus was to die, the religious leaders would have to convince the Roman leaders that He was a criminal. The next three trials of Jesus would be with the Roman leaders.

Truth: Jesus was not guilty of any wrongdoing.

Discuss:

1. Did the Sanhedrin keep the rules for a fair trial?

2. What did the Sanhedrin want the Messiah to do for them?

3. Of what did the Sanhedrin have to convince the Roman leaders?

Memorize: Week 3—Acts 2:32-33

• **Day 15—Acts 2:32**

³²This Jesus God raised up, and of that we all are witnesses. ³³ *Being therefore exalted at the right hand of God, and having received from the Father the promise of the Holy Spirit, he has poured out this that you yourselves are seeing and hearing.*

• **Discuss verse 32:**
"This Jesus"

Sing: "Up from the Grave He Arose" (p. 64)

• **Discuss "foes" (in the physical and spiritual realm).**
Who are Jesus' foes and how did He triumph over His foes?

Read: John 18:28-38

Listen: The Sanhedrin met again early that morning to finalize the decision that Jesus was guilty of blasphemy (Mark 15:1). The punishment for blasphemy was death, but the religious leaders did not have the authority to carry out the death penalty. The right to carry out the death penalty belonged to the Roman government. However Pilate, the Roman governor of Jerusalem, did not care that Jesus said He was the Messiah.

To get Pilate's attention the religious leaders had to make it seem that Jesus was guilty of breaking the Roman law. They told Pilate that Jesus did not pay taxes. Then they told Pilate that Jesus said He was a king (Luke 23:2). They knew Pilate did not want anyone other than himself to rule over the people.

Pilate asked Jesus questions but did not find any laws that Jesus had disobeyed. Jesus told Pilate that He was a king but His kingdom was different from the kingdoms of this world. Pilate did not know that he was talking with the real King of the universe, who had made everything. This was Pilate's chance to believe the truth about Jesus. Pilate was not too different from the religious leaders. He did not want to believe the truth about Jesus.

Truth: The truth about Jesus is that He is the Messiah-King.

Discuss:

1. Why did the Sanhedrin take Jesus to Pilate?

2. What opportunity did Jesus give to Pilate?

3. What is the truth about Jesus?

Memorize: Week 3–Acts 2:32-33

• **Day 16—Acts 2:32**

32This Jesus God raised up, and of that we all are witnesses. *33 Being therefore exalted at the right hand of God, and having received from the Father the promise of the Holy Spirit, he has poured out this that you yourselves are seeing and hearing.*

• **Discuss verse 32:**
"God raised up"

Sing: "Up from the Grave He Arose" (p. 64)

• **Discuss "mighty triumph" and "victor."**
When it seemed that Pilate was in control how was Jesus triumphant? How was Jesus the real victor during these trials?

Listen: Pilate wanted to let Jesus go free when he could not find any law that he had broken. However, Pilate knew that releasing Jesus would anger the religious leaders. When Pilate heard that Jesus used to live in the town of Galilee he sent Him to the government leader of Galilee named Herod. Pilate thought he had found the answer to his problem. Now Herod would be the one who had to make a decision about Jesus.

Herod was eager to meet Jesus. Herod hoped Jesus would perform a miracle for him. At an earlier time Jesus' cousin, John the Baptist, talked to Herod about God, but Herod did not like some of the things John taught. Herod put John the Baptist in prison and later had him killed (Mark 6:16-29). Why did Jesus not answer Herod's questions? Jesus knew Herod only wanted a miracle and did not want to know the truth about God. Herod did not listen to John and he would not listen to Jesus either.

Herod was angry that Jesus did not talk to him. Herod let his soldiers put a robe on Jesus to make fun of Him. The meeting with Herod was the fifth unfair trial for Jesus. He had not slept all night. His bruised body had been beaten and cut open. People had said bad things about Jesus and made fun of Him. After this, Herod sent Jesus back to Pilate.

Truth: Jesus was not guilty of any wrongdoing.

Discuss:

1. Who was Herod and what had he done to John the Baptist?

2. Why did Jesus not answer Herod's questions?

3. What caused Jesus to suffer during the trials?

Memorize: Week 3–Acts 2:32-33

• Day 17—Acts 2:32

32This Jesus God raised up, and of that we all are witnesses. 33 Being therefore exalted at the right hand of God, and having received from the Father the promise of the Holy Spirit, he has poured out this that you yourselves are seeing and hearing.

• Discuss verse 32:
"and of that we are all witnesses"

Sing: "Up from the Grave He Arose" (p. 64)

• Discuss "vainly."
What were all the attempts to stop God's plan? Why were all these attempts in vain?

Listen: Pilate was running out of ideas. He had sent Jesus to Herod, but Herod did not find any law that Jesus had disobeyed and sent Him back to Pilate. In all six trials, no one found any true reason for Jesus to die. Since Pilate was not a Jew, keeping the Jewish law did not matter to him. But he did want the Jewish religious leaders to like him. If he did not do what they wanted, they would complain about him. Pilate cared more about himself than about doing what was right.

Pilate was pleased to think of one more idea that might help him. Every year during Passover, the people could choose one prisoner to release from prison (Mark 15:6). A prisoner named Barabbas was a robber and had killed people. Pilate was sure the people knew that Barabbas deserved to die for his many crimes, and he believed that the people would want Barabbas to stay in prison and Jesus to go free. But the people chose Barabbas to go free. Pilate had Jesus beaten before letting the people kill him.

Barabbas did many bad things yet was set free to live. And Jesus who did nothing wrong was taken away to die. Like Barabbas, we have all sinned and deserve punishment for our sin (Rom. 6:23). Like Barabbas, we can be set free (saved from hell and set free to live forever with God) because Jesus died in our place. Jesus took God's punishment for our sin.

Truth: Jesus died even though He had done nothing wrong.

Discuss:

1. What did Pilate hope would happen with Barabbas and Jesus?

2. How are we like Barabbas?

3. What did Jesus do for us? Have you thanked Jesus?

Memorize: Week 3–Acts 2:32-33

• **Day 18—Acts 2:33**

32This Jesus God raised up, and of that we all are witnesses. **33 Being therefore exalted at the right hand of God, and having received from the Father the promise of the Holy Spirit, he has poured out this that you yourselves are seeing and hearing.**

• **Discuss verse 33:**
"Being therefore exalted"

Sing: "Up from the Grave He Arose" (p. 64)

• **Discuss "Jesus my Savior."**
What is the difference between saying, "Jesus is the Savior" and "Jesus is my Savior"?

Listen: Jesus was badly beaten. The soldiers twisted a branch with long sharp thorns into a circle and pressed this "crown" down on His head. The cuts on Jesus' back made it too hard for Him to carry the heavy cross. A man named Simon had to carry Jesus' cross.

They nailed Jesus to the cross. Pilate put a sign above Jesus that read: "The King of the Jews." As hard as the Roman leaders tried, they could not find any reason for Jesus to die. So they decided to punish Jesus for saying He was a king. The Roman leaders did not want any kings to stir up a rebellion of the people against the Roman government. But they knew Jesus was not leading anyone to rebel against the Roman government.

Why did the sign read "King of the Jews" in three different languages? People speaking different languages were in Jerusalem to celebrate the Passover. Although the people spoke different languages each person understood at least one of the three languages on the sign (John 19:20). People thought Jesus was being killed because He had led a rebellion against the Roman government.

The religious leaders and even the people walking by yelled at Jesus. They told Him to come down from the cross and save Himself if He really was the Messiah-King. Jesus could have come down from the cross. But Jesus wanted to do what God planned. God planned for Jesus to die to take the punishment for sin. Jesus could have saved Himself, but because of His love, He wanted to save us from having to take the awful punishment for our sin.

Truth: Jesus obeyed God's plan to take the punishment for sin.

Discuss:

1. What happened when Jesus could not carry the cross?

2. Why were people speaking different languages in Jerusalem?

3. Why did Jesus stay on the cross when He could have come down?

Memorize: Week 3–Acts 2:32-33

• Day 19—Acts 2:33

³²*This Jesus God raised up, and of that we all are witnesses.* **³³ Being therefore exalted at the right hand of God, and having received from the Father the promise of the Holy Spirit, he has poured out this that you yourselves are seeing and hearing.**

• Discuss verse 33:
"at the right hand of God"

Sing: "Up from the Grave He Arose" (p. 64)

• Discuss "reign" from "lives forever with His saints to reign."
What does it mean that Jesus lives forever to reign as King over His universe?

READ: LUKe 23:32-43

WEEK 3 · DAY 20

Listen: Two criminals were nailed to crosses on either side of Jesus. They had stolen things and killed people. The punishment for their crimes was death.

One of the criminals knew Jesus was going to heaven. He wanted to go to heaven too, but he knew that was not possible because he had committed evil crimes. How could a holy God who does not have any sin ever accept a person with so much sin? The criminal knew he needed God's forgiveness. Jesus told the man he would be in heaven that very day. Going to heaven and living forever with Jesus is a gift that brings more happiness than any other gift you can imagine. The other criminal did not fear God or trust Jesus. He would not be in heaven. Living forever in hell apart from Jesus brings more sadness than any other pain. Taking the punishment for one's own sin, in hell, forever, is worse than any other punishment.

Are there sins that are too big to be forgiven? When a person is truly sad about his sin and wants to stop sinning, he can ask for God's forgiveness. God promises to forgive no matter what the sin. How can God forgive our sin when we have not taken the punishment we deserve? God thinks of our sin as belonging to Jesus who took the punishment in our place. Then God thinks of Jesus' sinless life as belonging to us (Rom 5:1). Can you believe how wonderful this is? As a person trusts in Jesus, it is as if God takes off his or her dirty clothes of sin and puts on a beautiful spotless robe of Jesus' righteousness (Isa. 61:10).

Truth: God welcomes into heaven all who have trusted Jesus for forgiveness.

Discuss:

1. Why were the criminals crucified?

2. Why did Jesus tell the one criminal that he would go to heaven?

3. What happens to a person who trusts Jesus and asks for forgiveness?

Memorize: Week 3–Acts 2:32-33

• Day 20—Acts 2:33

³²This Jesus God raised up, and of that we all are witnesses. **³³ Being therefore exalted at the right hand of God, and having received from the Father the promise of the Holy Spirit, he has poured out this that you yourselves are seeing and hearing.**

• Discuss verse 33:
"having received from the Father the promise of the Holy Spirit"

Sing: "Up from the Grave He Arose" (p. 64)

• Discuss "prey."
How was death not able to hold on to Jesus and the criminal who believed?

44 · WEEK 3 DAY 20

WHY EASTER?

Listen: On the night Jesus was born, a very bright star lit up the sky like day. On the day Jesus died, the sky became dark as night. Jesus was nailed to the cross in the morning (Mark 15:25). At midday when the sun is usually the brightest, it became dark. God made the sun stop shining for three hours. God who has complete control over the sun, moon, and stars wanted people to know how much He hates sin.

There is no one like God. He is powerful and holy. Sin is never okay with God and He is right to punish sin. At the same time, God is merciful. That means He is kind to us when we do not deserve it. In His mercy God made a way to save us from death and hell so we can be in heaven and live with Him forever. Does that mean He just forgets about our punishment? Is God like a father who says, "I guess I will let it go this time"? If God let sin go without punishment, He would not be holy and just. God does not forget about our punishment. Jesus took the punishment for us. Because Jesus always obeyed God's commands and never sinned, He was able to take our place. As Jesus hung on the cross, He took all the fierce anger and powerful hatred that God has toward sin. And Jesus experienced a kind of pain greater than all the rest when the Father distanced Himself (Mark15:34).

Because of God's love and kindness, He planned for Jesus to be your substitute. And because of Jesus' love for you He obeyed the Father's plan. What did Jesus mean when He said, "It is finished" (John 19:30)? Jesus meant that He had finished taking all the punishment for our sin. Jesus loves you. He was punished in your place.

Truth: Jesus died on the cross, taking all the punishment for sin.

Discuss:

1. What happened to the sun on the day Jesus died?

2. What does it mean that God is merciful?

3. What did Jesus finish when He was on the cross?

Memorize: Week 3–Acts 2:32-33

• **Day 21—Acts 2:33**

32This Jesus God raised up, and of that we all are witnesses. 33 Being therefore exalted at the right hand of God, and having received from the Father the promise of the Holy Spirit, he has poured out this that you yourselves are seeing and hearing.

• **Discuss verse 33:**
"he has poured out this that you yourselves are seeing and hearing"

Sing: "Up from the Grave He Arose" (p. 64)

• **Discuss "waiting the coming day."**
What was the "coming day" for Jesus?

Listen: When the full punishment for sin was finished Jesus took His last breath and let go of life on earth. At the time when Jesus died, the curtain in the temple was torn in half. Why was there a curtain in the temple?

The curtain was in a special room of the temple called the Most Holy Place. The long and thick curtain divided this room from all the other rooms in the temple (Ex. 26:33). One day every year the high priest went into this special room with the blood of a lamb and asked God to forgive the people's sins. Only the high priest could come into God's presence, and only with the blood of the lamb. Because of God's love and mercy, He allowed a lamb to die in place of the people who had sinned. Boys and girls at that time may not have understood this very well, but when they believed God and trusted Him to forgive them, He did.

The curtain was too thick to cut with a sharp knife so how did it tear open? And how did the long curtain tear from top to bottom? God tore the curtain. Why did God do this? God tore the curtain to tell us that through the death of Jesus the way for us to come to God was now open (John 14:6). We no longer need the high priest to take the blood of a lamb into the Most Holy Place of the temple. Now each person can come to God through the blood of Jesus. Each of us can ask God to forgive our sin and He will (Heb. 9:23-28).

Truth: Jesus opened the way for us to come to God.

Discuss:

1. Why was there a curtain in the temple?

2. Why did God tear the curtain?

3. Who can come to God?

Memorize: Week 4–Acts 2:36-39

• **Day 22—Acts 2:36**

36 "Let all the house of Israel therefore know for certain that God has made him both Lord and Christ, this Jesus whom you crucified." 37 Now when they heard this they were cut to the heart, and said to Peter and the rest of the apostles, "Brothers, what shall we do?" 38 And Peter said to them, "Repent and be baptized every one of you in the name of Jesus Christ for the forgiveness of your sins, and you will receive the gift of the Holy Spirit. 39 For the promise is for you and for your children and for all who are far off, everyone whom the Lord our God calls to himself."

• **Discuss verse 36:**
"Let all the house of Israel therefore know for certain that God has made him both Lord and Christ, this Jesus whom you crucified."

Sing: "Thine Be the Glory" (p. 65)

• **Discuss "endless victory."**
How is Jesus' victory over death endless?

Read: Matthew 27:57-61

Listen: Long before Jesus died the prophet Isaiah said that Jesus' body would be buried in the tomb of a rich man. Isaiah 53:9 says: "He was assigned a grave with the wicked, and with the rich in his death, though he had done no violence, nor was any deceit in his mouth." When the words of a prophet actually happen, we learn that God is powerful and can do everything He promises to do. God was in control of all the events of Jesus' death.

Not all the religious leaders hated Jesus. A religious leader named Joseph of Arimathea believed Jesus was telling the truth when He said He was the Messiah. After Jesus died, Joseph asked Pilate for Jesus' body. Most bodies of people who died on a cross were thrown away without being buried in a grave. Joseph wanted to honor Jesus by wrapping His body in a special cloth and putting it in a new tomb. This was a burial that only a rich person could afford. Joseph was a rich man who could buy a tomb no one had ever used. After Joseph put Jesus' body in the tomb, he rolled a large stone, one too heavy to lift, over the opening.

Through the prophets, God told us many truths about the birth and death of Jesus long before Jesus came to earth. When prophecy actually happens, we learn that God's Word is true. God has a plan and He has the power to make His plan happen. Joseph did not know it, but through him, God was fulfilling His Word about Jesus' death.

Truth: Jesus was buried according to God's plan.

Discuss:

1. Who was Joseph and what did he believe about Jesus?

2. What did Joseph do with Jesus' body?

3. What do we learn about God through fulfilled prophecy?

Memorize: Week 4–Acts 2:36-39

• **Day 23—Acts 2:37**

[36]"Let all the house of Israel therefore know for certain that God has made him both Lord and Christ, this Jesus whom you crucified." [37]**Now when they heard this they were cut to the heart, and said to Peter and the rest of the apostles, "Brothers, what shall we do?"** [38]And Peter said to them, "Repent and be baptized every one of you in the name of Jesus Christ for the forgiveness of your sins, and you will receive the gift of the Holy Spirit. [39]For the promise is for you and for your children and for all who are far off, everyone whom the Lord our God calls to himself."

• **Discuss verse 37:**
"Now when they heard this they were cut to the heart"

Sing: "Thine Be the Glory" (p. 65)

• **Discuss "glory" (worshipful praise, honor, and thanksgiving).**
How did Jesus receive glory?

Read: matthew 27:62-66

Listen: Jesus told people many times that He was going to die and then come to life again, but no one really believed Him. Even His closest friends, the disciples, did not understand this truth. However, the religious leaders who hated Him, remembered that Jesus said He would be buried for three days and come to life again (Matt. 12:38-40). They thought the disciples might come and take Jesus' dead body out of the tomb so they could say He had come back to life. The religious leaders did not want people to believe that Jesus had the power to come to life again. That would prove Jesus was not blasphemous but was the Messiah-King.

A large heavy stone already blocked the opening of the tomb, but the religious leaders added a seal to make sure the stone was not moved. The leaders were so afraid of what would happen if Jesus' body left the tomb that a guard kept watch day and night. They made it impossible for anyone to steal Jesus' body. No one could have taken Jesus' body from the tomb. Only God's power could raise Jesus to life and free Him from the tomb.

Truth: Jesus was raised to life by God's power.

Discuss:

1. What did the religious leaders think might happen to Jesus' body?

2. Why did they want to seal and guard the grave of Jesus?

3. Would it have been possible for anyone to steal the body of Jesus?

Memorize: Week 4–Acts 2:36-39

• **Day 24—Acts 2:37**

*36"Let all the house of Israel therefore know for certain that God has made him both Lord and Christ, this Jesus whom you crucified." 37**Now when they heard this they were cut to the heart, and said to Peter and the rest of the apostles, "Brothers, what shall we do?"** 38And Peter said to them, "Repent and be baptized every one of you in the name of Jesus Christ for the forgiveness of your sins, and you will receive the gift of the Holy Spirit. 39For the promise is for you and for your children and for all who are far off, everyone whom the Lord our God calls to himself."*

• **Discuss verse 37:**

"and said to Peter and the rest of the apostles, 'Brothers what shall we do?' "

Sing: "Thine Be the Glory" (p. 65)

• **Discuss "glorious Prince of Life; life is naught without thee."**
What does it mean that our life is nothing without the Prince of Life?

Listen: When have you been afraid? Mary Magdalene and another woman named Mary, along with the guards, were at Jesus' tomb. All of the sudden the earth started shaking so hard and they began shaking with fear. Did you notice who else was shaking? The guards started shaking and then they fainted. Were they afraid of the power of God? Were they afraid of the angel? Or were they afraid of what would happen to them when Pilate heard about this?

Why were the women afraid? They came to the tomb expecting to see the dead body of Jesus. Instead, they saw an angel as bright as a flash of lightning in the dim morning light. No human being could have moved the heavy stone and yet the angel made it look easy. Then the angel spoke and told them the best news they had ever heard. Jesus was no longer dead. Jesus was no longer in the tomb. Jesus was alive. With the stone rolled away, the women could look in the tomb and see that Jesus was not there.

As the women ran to tell the disciples what they had seen, Jesus met them. He really was alive! Now they knew that everything Jesus told them was true. Jesus is the Son of God, the Messiah-King. He really did finish taking all the punishment for our sin. When Jesus talked with Mary Magdalene and the other Mary, He said they must not be afraid any longer. Their fear turned to joyful trust in Jesus.

Truth: Jesus was raised from death to life.

Discuss:

1. Why were the guards so afraid?

2. What did the women see when they looked in the tomb?

3. What did the women know to be true about Jesus?

Memorize: Week 4–Acts 2:36-39

• Day 25—Acts 2:38

36"*Let all the house of Israel therefore know for certain that God has made him both Lord and Christ, this Jesus whom you crucified.*" 37*Now when they heard this they were cut to the heart, and said to Peter and the rest of the apostles, "Brothers, what shall we do?"* 38***And Peter said to them, "Repent and be baptized every one of you in the name of Jesus Christ for the forgiveness of your sins, and you will receive the gift of the Holy Spirit.*** 39*For the promise is for you and for your children and for all who are far off, everyone whom the Lord our God calls to himself.*"

• Discuss verse 38:

"And Peter said to them, 'Repent and be baptized every one of you in the name of Jesus Christ for the forgiveness of your sins'"

Sing: "Thine Be the Glory" (p. 65)

• Discuss "scatters fear and gloom."

How did Jesus scatter away fear and gloom for the women?

Read: Luke 24:13–35

Listen: Cleopas and his friend were sad and confused. If Jesus really was the Messiah-King, why did He die? And why did the women not find Jesus' body when they went to the tomb? Was it just a dream that an angel had told them that Jesus was alive? The more Cleopas and his friend talked the more questions they had.

And who was this man that was walking with them? Why did he not know what had happened? Everybody in Jerusalem for the Passover knew that Jesus of Nazareth was crucified. They could not hide their sadness and confusion as they told this man the story. However, when the stranger started explaining from the Scriptures God's plan for the Messiah-King, it all started to make sense. Did they learn that Jesus was the prophet Moses said would come (Deut. 18:15)? Did they realize that Isaiah had told about the crucifixion (Isa. 53)? Did they understand that the Psalms spoke of the resurrection (Ps. 16:10)? For the first time it became clear to them that everything happened to Jesus just as God had planned.

When Cleopas and his friend realized that this person walking and talking with them was Jesus, they were happier than they had ever been. Now they were certain that Jesus was alive and that He was the Messiah-King. When Jesus came back to life, it proved He was God. Only God has the power to give life to the dead. One day the body of everyone who believes in Jesus will be raised to life from where they have been buried (1 Cor. 15:42-43). God made sure that many people saw Jesus after He came back to life, so we know it really happened. Cleopas and his friend were just two of over 500 people who saw Jesus, with their own eyes, after He died and came back to life (1 Cor. 15:6).

Truth: Jesus was raised from the dead and is alive.

Discuss:

1. What are some questions you still have about Jesus?

2. What does the Old Testament tell us about Jesus?

3. Why did God make sure that many people saw that Jesus was alive?

Memorize: Week 4–Acts 2:36-39

- **Day 26—Acts 2:38**

36"Let all the house of Israel therefore know for certain that God has made him both Lord and Christ, this Jesus whom you crucified." 37Now when they heard this they were cut to the heart, and said to Peter and the rest of the apostles, "Brothers, what shall we do?" 38**And Peter said to them, "Repent and be baptized every one of you in the name of Jesus Christ for the forgiveness of your sins, and you will receive the gift of the Holy Spirit.** 39For the promise is for you and for your children and for all who are far off, everyone whom the Lord our God calls to himself."

- **Discuss verse 38:**
"and you will receive the gift of the Holy Spirit"

Sing: "Thine Be the Glory" (p. 65)

- **Discuss "no more we doubt thee."**
When did Cleopas and his friend stop doubting Jesus?

Listen: Jesus' friends, the disciples, remembered that during their last supper together Jesus had said, "After I have risen, I will go ahead of you into Galilee" (Matt. 26:32). However, it was frightening to think that those who killed Jesus might kill them too. Should they go? Would it be worth it to travel all the way to Galilee if Jesus was not alive? Then after the women returned from the tomb, they told the disciples that Jesus was alive and that He had said to them "Do not be afraid. Go and tell my brothers to go to Galilee; there they will see me" (Matt. 28:10).

There was new hope in the disciples' hearts as they set off for the long journey to Galilee. It took several days to get there but every step of the journey meant they were closer to seeing Jesus once again. When they reached the mountain and saw Jesus, nothing else in life mattered. They knew He was God and fell down to worship the only One worthy of honor and praise.

The disciples listened closely to every word as Jesus told them what to do next. Jesus said they were to go and help other people to become disciples of Jesus. What is a disciple? A disciple is a person who believes Jesus is the Son of God. A disciple trusts in the work of Jesus to forgive his or her sin. A disciple is made spiritually alive because Jesus has given His Spirit to live within him or her. By the power of Jesus' Spirit within him, a disciple can obey God and say "no" to sin. A disciple becomes Jesus' friend. A disciple makes other disciples by teaching people how to love and obey Jesus.

Truth: Jesus wants His friends to go and make other disciples.

Discuss:

1. Where did the disciples meet Jesus?

2. What does it mean to be a disciple of Jesus?

3. What command did Jesus give to every disciple?

Memorize: Week 4–Acts 2:36-39

• Day 27—Acts 2:39

36"Let all the house of Israel therefore know for certain that God has made him both Lord and Christ, this Jesus whom you crucified." 37Now when they heard this they were cut to the heart, and said to Peter and the rest of the apostles, "Brothers, what shall we do?" 38And Peter said to them, "Repent and be baptized every one of you in the name of Jesus Christ for the forgiveness of your sins, and you will receive the gift of the Holy Spirit. **39For the promise is for you and for your children and for all who are far off, everyone whom the Lord our God calls to himself."**

• Discuss verse 39:

"For the promise is for you and for your children and for all who are far off"

Sing: "Thine Be the Glory" (p. 65)

• Discuss "risen conquering Son."

How is Jesus' victory over death important for His disciples today?

Listen: Where is Jesus now? Is He in heaven or with us? Why are we not able to see Jesus? Is Jesus coming back?

If Jesus told the disciples to go out into the whole world and make disciples, why did He tell them to wait in Jerusalem? They had to wait for the Holy Spirit. If they went out without the Holy Spirit they would not have God's power to help people to believe what they said.

Though Jesus was going back to live in Heaven with His Father, He sent His Spirit to live within each person who is His disciple (Acts 1:5). Jesus' Spirit (the Holy Spirit) gives courage and power to tell other people about Him (Acts 1:8). The Holy Spirit helps a disciple understand God's Word (John 16:13). The Holy Spirit gives a disciple help to do whatever God asks (Eph. 3:16, 20). Who is the Holy Spirit? The Holy Spirit is God (Matt.28:19).

In heaven, Jesus is with His Father in His resurrected body. On earth Jesus is with us in His Spirit—the Holy Spirit. Jesus' Spirit lives within each person who is His disciple (1 Cor 6:19-20). We cannot see Jesus' Spirit today because the Holy Spirit is not visible. However, one day Jesus will return in His body and everyone will be able to see Him (Matt.24:30). Jesus told His disciples to always be ready for His return which could be at any time (Matt. 24:42). Until Jesus returns, we are to tell others about Him so they also can believe in Him.

Truth: Jesus is coming again!

Discuss:

1. Why did Jesus tell the disciples to wait in Jerusalem?

2. Where is Jesus today?

3. What did Jesus tell His disciples to do until He returns?

Memorize: Week 4–Acts 2:36-39

• Day 28—Acts 2:39

[36]"Let all the house of Israel therefore know for certain that God has made him both Lord and Christ, this Jesus whom you crucified." [37]Now when they heard this they were cut to the heart, and said to Peter and the rest of the apostles, "Brothers, what shall we do?" [38]And Peter said to them, "Repent and be baptized every one of you in the name of Jesus Christ for the forgiveness of your sins, and you will receive the gift of the Holy Spirit. [39]**For the promise is for you and for your children and for all who are far off, everyone whom the Lord our God calls to himself."**

• Discuss verse 39:
"everyone whom the Lord our God calls to himself."

Sing: "Thine Be the Glory" (p. 65)

• Discuss "death has lost its sting."
How has death lost its sting now that Jesus is alive?

song for week 1: "when I survey the wondrous cross"

by Isaac Watts, 1707

When I survey the wondrous cross
On which the Prince of Glory died,
My richest gain I count but loss,
And pour contempt on all my pride.

Forbid it, Lord, that I should boast,
Save in the death of Christ my God!
All the vain things that charm me most,
I sacrifice them to His blood.

See from His head, His hands, His feet,
Sorrow and love flow mingled down!
Did e'er such love and sorrow meet,
Or thorns compose so rich a crown?

Were the whole realm of nature mine,
That were a present far too small;
Love so amazing, so divine,
Demands my soul, my life, my all.

song for week 2: "Man of Sorrows! what a Name"

by Philip P. Bliss, 1875

"Man of Sorrows!" what a name
For the Son of God, who came
Ruined sinners to reclaim.
Hallelujah! What a Savior!

Bearing shame and scoffing rude,
In my place condemned He stood;
Sealed my pardon with His blood.
Hallelujah! What a Savior!

Guilty, vile, and helpless we;
Spotless Lamb of God was He;
"Full atonement!" can it be?
Hallelujah! What a Savior!

Lifted up was He to die;
"It is finished!" was His cry;
Now in Heav'n exalted high.
Hallelujah! What a Savior!

When He comes, our glorious King,
All His ransomed home to bring,
Then anew His song we'll sing:
Hallelujah! What a Savior!

song for week 3: "up from the grave He Arose"

by Robert Lowry, 1874

Low in the grave He lay,

Jesus my Savior,

Waiting the coming day,

Jesus my Lord!

Refrain:

Up from the grave He arose,

With a mighty triumph o'er His foes,

He arose a Victor from the dark domain,

And He lives forever, with His saints to reign.

He arose! He arose!

Hallelujah! Christ arose!

Vainly they watch His bed,

Jesus my Savior;

Vainly they seal the dead,

Jesus my Lord!

Refrain

Death cannot keep its Prey,

Jesus my Savior;

He tore the bars away,

Jesus my Lord!

Refrain

Song for Week 4: "Thine Be the Glory"

By Edmond L. Budry, 1884

Thine be the glory, risen, conquering Son;
Endless is the victory, Thou o'er death hast won;
Angels in bright raiment rolled the stone away,
Kept the folded grave clothes where Thy body lay.

Refrain:

Thine is the glory, risen conquering Son,
Endless is the victory, Thou o'er death hast won.

Lo! Jesus meets us, risen from the tomb;
Lovingly He greets us, scatters fear and gloom;
Let the church with gladness, hymns of triumph sing;
For her Lord now liveth, death hath lost its sting.

Refrain

No more we doubt Thee, glorious Prince of life;
Life is naught without Thee; aid us in our strife;
Make us more than conquerors, through Thy deathless love:
Bring us safe through Jordan to Thy home above.

Refrain

Acknowledgments

My heart is full of gratitude for my husband Ron. We are co-laborers in the cause of Christ and the model of his Christ-like life is a great blessing to our grandchildren.

I am grateful for my son Dr. Benjamin Reaoch who contributed as the spiritual editor of this work.

How thankful I am for my sister Carol McCarty whose illustrations flowed from her heart of worship to God.

I am grateful for the ministry of Bible Study Fellowship through which I have learned the joy of engaging with God in His Word.

For my dear friends Paul and Evie Bowers I give thanks. Their contribution of thorough editing, suggestions and prayer has proven invaluable.

Lastly, I want to thank the parents of our grandchildren – Ben, Stacy, Chris, and Elizabeth. It is a joy to watch them give their children the gift of loving and consistent spiritual instruction.

About the Author

Barbara Reaoch is Bible Study Fellowship International's Director of children's programs. For nearly twenty years, she taught women's BSF classes in the U.S. and South Africa. Barbara also worked at the Rafiki Girl's Center in South Africa, teaching the Bible and life skills to young women. She has been married to Ron for forty years; they have three grown children and four grandchildren.